Carol Deering's poems are exceedingly well made. They are lyrical, concise, and filled with memorable imagery. The poet herself is perceptive, humane, and eloquent. The publication of this collection is a welcome and noteworthy event. Here is a book that should be read many times over and deeply appreciated for its own sake.
—N. Scott Momaday, Kiowa writer of fiction, essays, and poetry, is the Pulitzer Prize-winning author of House Made of Dawn.

In her impressive debut collection, Havoc & Solace, *Carol Deering celebrates the inland West. Ecstatic and luminous, her poems construct a "tracery of awe" in that intersection between the self and the natural world: sunrise and dew, the coyote and the meadowlark, lightning on the horizon and "little moons reflecting in our eyes." Cognizant of the "brittle" world and the tenuousness of peace, these are poems of witness, wonder and revelation, poems that rejoice in the act of looking carefully and intensely until "all the senses ring."*
—James McKean earned his MFA from the University of Iowa Writers' Workshop and his Ph.D. from the University of Iowa. He is the author of three books of poetry: Headlong, Tree of Heaven, and We Are the Bus.

From poignant encounters with wild creatures to vivid evocations of Western landscapes and people, Carol makes magic with words.
—Lynne Bama, an award-winning poet and journalist, is the author of Yellowstone Rising.

We love her voice and think it's an important one to share.
—The Crow Literary Journal, editor Joy Austin.

Havoc and Solace *is an ode to place, Wyoming and the American West, where "[f]ences wear wild grapes and roses" and "[t]arpaper farmhouses / flap to the beat of a breeze." Deering's spaces are vast and intimate, sacred and inhabited by all manner of wildlife: deer, coyote, cattle, elk, bison, bear, mayflies, a spotted fawn, pronghorn, rabbits, rattlesnake, lizard, packrat, "lambs and wolf pups," and so many birds! We feel Deering's love for the land and her fear for its future. These highly condensed imagistic poems are utterly devoid of sentiment, cliché or any sense of straining to sound poetic. I so appreciate Deering's rigorous restraint and complete absence of poetic self-consciousness! "Angle of Incidence" ends in a powerful but vulnerable place where "little birds on roadside stalks / rise and shiver to a mist / shying me to tears." It takes a lot to earn an ending like that, but Deering pulls it off again and again in spare free-verse poems that, delicate and vital, feel like sculpted air.*

—Rebecca Foust, Marin County Poet Laureate and author of *Paradise Drive*, winner of the Press 53 Award for Poetry.

HAVOC & SOLACE

HAVOC & SOLACE

Poems from the Inland West

by

Carol L. Deering

Edited by
Lori Howe

Sastrugi Press

Copyright © 2018 by Carol L. Deering

Sastrugi Press / Published by arrangement with the author

Havoc & Solace: Poems from the Inland West

All rights reserved. No part of this publication may be distributed, reproduced, or transmitted in any form or by any means, including recording, photocopying, or other electronic or mechanical methods, without the prior written permission of the publisher, except in the case of brief quotations embodied in critical reviews and certain other noncommercial uses permitted by copyright law. For permission requests, write to the publisher, addressed "Attention: Permissions Coordinator," at the address below.

Sastrugi Press
PO Box 1297, Jackson, WY 83001, United States
www.sastrugipress.com

Library of Congress Catalog-in-Publication Data
Library of Congress Control Number: 2018960660
Deering, Carol L.
Havoc and Solace / 1st United States edition
p. cm.
1. Poetry 2. Poetry, American 3. Poetry—Women Authors 4. Poets—Wyoming
Summary: This collection of poetry by Carol Deering takes the reader into the beautiful yet harsh world of the American inland West.

ISBN-13: 978-1-944986-46-9 (paperback), 978-1-944986-53-7 (hardback)

Cover images ©2018 Aaron Linsdau

PS3604.E44 H38 2018
811.6 Dee
Printed in the United States of America

10 9 8 7 6 5 4 3 2 1

For Andy, for everything

The quote on page 1 by Paul Bransom is from **Bob Kuhn: Drawing on Instinct**, Adam Duncan and James McNutt, Eds. (University of Oklahoma Press, 2012), p. 23. Used with permission of the University of Oklahoma Press.

The quote on page 28 by Terry Tempest Williams is from "America's National Parks: By Definition," from **The Hour of Land: A Personal Topography of America's National Parks**, by Terry Tempest Williams. Copyright © 2016 by Terry Tempest Williams. Reprinted by permission of Farrar, Straus and Giroux.

The quote on page 55 by Naomi Shihab Nye is from her poem "White Hair over the Rocky Mountains," in **Red Suitcase: Poems** (BOA Editions, Ltd., 1994), pp. 29-30. Used with permission of Naomi Shihab Nye.

CONTENTS

Big, Dark Eyes Asking Who, What, Why All at Once	**1**
A Few Seconds Eye-To-Eye	2
Let It Be	3
Stopping at Louis Lake	4
Interchange, Wyoming	6
Twilight, Angus	8
Quill Shine	9
Homespun	11
Phrynosoma Douglassii	12
Alchemy	13
Whenever I Brake for Deer	14
A Flurry of Horses	16
Daybreak, Jackson Lake	17
Leupp Road Crossing	19
Call & Response	20
The Air Is Fresh & Wild	21
Squall at Fishing Bridge	23
Free To Roam	24
Mayfly Destiny	25
The Brittle World	26
I Rest among the Pebble Beds, My Hair in Loose Raceme	**28**
In an Abandoned Greenhouse	29
Daylily Pastorale	30
The Blossom of This Air	31

Natural History	32
Codge 'n Sarah's Mercantile	33
I'll Take Your Silence	35
Like a Spirited Summer Creek	36
To You, Lake Yellowstone	38
Nebraska Daydream	39
Magical Riff	40
The Falls	41
This Day	43
In a Desert Fastness	44
On the Trail	45
Paper Birch	46
Popo Agie Palette	47
Down at Troublesome Creek	48
Helianthus, Hozho	49
Blue Sky Highway	50
Reminiscence	51
Stories on the Wind	52
Midnight, March	54

Dirt, Our Common Skin, Our Rich Identity in Space	**55**
We Named Our Planet	56
Nevada Sands	57
Light Physics	58
Navajo Moon	59
The August West	60
We Were the Purple Distance	61
Indian Ricegrass	64
Mud Bubbles & Breathes	65

In the Balance	67
Dawn to Dusk, a Lifespan	69
Broken Weave	70
Harvest Whimsy	71
Somewhere West of Laramie	72
Angle of Incidence	73
Passage	74
The Same Wind, Light & Restless Rain	75
The Mile-High West	77
Wind's Apology	78
ACKNOWLEDGEMENTS	79
NOTES	81
THANKS	83
ABOUT THE AUTHOR	84

"BIG DARK EYES ASKING WHO, WHAT, WHY ALL AT ONCE"

"When you look at an animal, look at it as though you may never see it again."

Paul Bransom

Carol L. Deering

A FEW SECONDS EYE-TO-EYE

Licking branches and fallen seeds,
tasting the air by the color-blown
flower patch, stalking ancestral trails,
the does outside my window

> *big dark eyes asking who, what,*
> *why all at once*

flow like phantoms in the dusk.

Birdfeeders sway, dark lanterns
against the flick of white tails.

LET IT BE

A great blue heron
shone among the cattails
at the brink of the pond,
tall and still as a chalice,
only twice in several minutes
turning its dark-plumed head.

But half a dozen blackbirds
from a horde of dozens more

kept harassing
      mobbing
   jabbing   towards it,
     wishing it ill.

Slowly it swooped its luxurious wings

    drew in its resplendent head

        trailed back its streamer-ribbon legs,

            rose and drifted past the hill,

                irrepressible as spring.

Carol L. Deering

STOPPING AT LOUIS LAKE

    We took the Loop Road,
the long way. We had endless time.

New to Wyoming, driving to a dinner
in my husband's honor, a welcoming, we

rounded a curve and there *he* was.
All our journeys out of mind.

A moose, a prince
dining, deep in the water, in the light

we inhaled, his body dark and silky, dripping lake
and luxurious grace

the lungs of the night calling,
droplets spilling rings from his dewlap

in a rhythm we could live on, each time
he raised his weighty head.

Twilight settled over us,
the immediacy of dark pines, his

presence, and our watching.
Nimbly his long legs drew him

backwards-jointed to the bank,
where he began to nibble dusk.

    We were late. The inn
had food prepared family-style

now on ice or back burners. We
were served crustily. The moose

never left us…

    Our welcoming.

Carol L. Deering

INTERCHANGE, WYOMING

Beyond the sage and pale
sparse grasses,
      he posed atop a hill

long-legged against the sky,
watching our pickup
      slow, back up, and turn

onto a two-track dusty trail,
drawn
      inescapably to him.

Somewhere in the wilds
between Farson and Kemmerer
      we stopped to gaze upon

a wolf. He turned us over
in his mind. *All the history,*
      merciless humanity

the stigma of "big bad,"
upheaval, removal,
      traps and loss.

Havoc & Solace

What this rolling red machine might cause.

Then, as though he etched a line
parting civilized
       and free

as though our brush with wonder
proved unworthy
       of his time

he turned away
ritually

       sustaining the divide.

Carol L. Deering

TWILIGHT, ANGUS

They chew up this edge of the pasture,
ripping stitches from the land.
Shadows, shaking their cloudlike breath,
lumber through irrigated grasses,
feeding on twilight's energy.

Time steers the horn-tipped moon
in paths worn through the sky.
Now and then a sonorous remark
journeys to odd corners of the night
where darkness flowers.

Legs on the offbeat, shifting
with stodgy ghostly grace,
dark cattle stir white clover

                stars.

QUILL SHINE

The other day, right by my door,
a porcupine, loose prickly hair,
slogged in a rollicky,   drowsy,
self-absorbed stride
searching for a spot   to doze outside.
She's quite at ease, this near
the house, as she must be,
to rule the night.

What looked like a twiggy nest
grew to golden radiance
in morning's tempered glare.

The porcupine's asleep up there,
in the elm beside the pond.

Sporadically she turns, and an arm
or a leg drags down. I watch
and wait, but miss her groggy trip
to the ground.

Carol L. Deering

       Sun
  nuzzles the pond to ripples
      all the lazy afternoon.

A different day, a cloudless drive,
a porcupine immobilized, guts and quills
on the dotted line,
closing out a loan.

       O thumbprint moon,
  quill-basket white
         with deep design,

    incite our fragile
tenancy   and our tenacity
    to shine.

HOMESPUN

Snow stirs a shiver of birds
past the uprooted moon, then settles
back within the sage. A whisk of skirts,
and a woman turns inward. Her breath
leaves the pane a blister of stars.
She moves in lantern shadows, silent,
scraping quills of ice from the chinks.
The baby sleeps in his packing crate.
Over the girls lie a braided rug,
wild blankets blossoming with frost.

What madness drove their dreams to wander
to a land where the wind was born?
The biting chill preys on her senses,
her fingers swollen raw. A spider's web
drapes awry, flaunting moths
like trinkets to the glass, spangles
fading in the storm. Such arrogance
from a frozen artisan – a weaver
like herself, poised in the tracery of awe.

Carol L. Deering

PHRYNOSOMA DOUGLASSII

Beneath the overcast
high altitude, it appears at my feet
in spiky camouflage

> like a pink and charcoal
> stone, sculpted
> of sunset-volcanic ash

> or an heirloom pocket watch
> in an extravagant case
> with tapering fob.

A short-horned lizard,
stubborn-looking head
with an outsized frown.

Gravity must weigh upon that mouth.

Stout horns, splotches
trailing a fringe of scales
down either side

braiding to a stumpy tail,
it spraddles friable cinders.
Then in a soundless burst

of tumult, its sturdy legs
begin to claw away. I jump back

> somehow in time as well as space

grasping the threat I am.

ALCHEMY

The fox on Riverview, beautiful
as he lay. Small pointed face,
black-tipped snout, white fur gesturing
in a paw's sweep of pathos,
his coat the colors of autumn
fading. Three magpies feasting,
his ribcage a nave.

The fox lay elegant, delicate
for days, until all carnage
rose.

     A swoon of leaves
rides down the wind. I doze
in my den, let images spin,
editing out
the raucous birds

lifting
     my forepaws,
stalking
     the foothills

for gold
     and tasty
     piñon-spirited
          words.

Carol L. Deering

WHENEVER I BRAKE FOR DEER

Nights on the bleak side
of violet, no streetlight for
miles. Survival on Riverview
can alter in a blink.

My arm shoots out across the seat
whenever I brake for deer.

I round a curve. A river
of does and young bucks
is slowing on the road. I slam my brakes
and reach across, but you of course
aren't here. I watch the deer,

the embers of their eyes sizing up
the circumstance, and after a breath
crossing the stage of my beams, off right.

I wait, knowing animals can straggle,
rush recklessly onto the road,
change their minds and turn back.

I've seen in daylight how they flow
jumping a fence, front legs
folded, some diving between the wires.
The last and youngest can pace

Havoc & Solace

alongside, indecisive, leap and settle
belly on the top barbed wire,
and rock for two terrible, interminable
seconds. Then, by sheer oomph
or prayer, thrust himself over,
his mother trembling,

powerless, except to care.

Sitting in darkness, viewing only
this small-lit world, I sense I'm free
to go. Free to slide my foot
to the gas. I draw up a primal faith,
believing as the velvet deer,
I'll find my way back home.

for Brandon

Carol L. Deering

A FLURRY OF HORSES

The clouds are molting. Feathers
tickle the horses, who can't stand
still. A soft nicker of sun

falls through the frosted spray.
The horses leap, swing their heads,
then sweep the periphery of joy.

DAYBREAK, JACKSON LAKE

Chilled, drizzly ambience,
pensive, preverbal.

We three, a choppy lake,
slog towards waffles at the lodge.

> A rattling disruption,
> the sound of lumber
> loose and falling
>
> a young moose
> scrabbling on river rocks
>
> scurries from his bed
> into the misty pines.

A sheet of ice shatters.
And every cell in my body
turns to its neighbor,
bows and steps apart.

Carol L. Deering

I am a constellation
glittering. All hearts

beat faster, after
a second's rupture:

      the droplets bracing

      prismatic, transparent,

      consuming our loose-limbed minds.

LEUPP ROAD CROSSING

Morning slices past our shoulders
as we ride to wake the wind.
Face-shield scratches fill
with skyline. Flash of killdeer,
flash of antelope, striped necks
scribbling on the light.

Sage rats peek from crumbling
pavement. Blue-green magpies
call and flee, foraging
cold breakfast plains. Words
spill into rushing pockets. Sky
tilts headlong on the curves.

Up ahead a tawny rippling.
A coyote, sprightly, regal,
lopes across the road,
then stops. Our hearts
downshift.

God's Dog turns full face,
golden red with flecks
of midnight, piercing
the gap
with neo-Miocene eyes
as we power up to fly.

Carol L. Deering

CALL & RESPONSE

As morning calls to a meadowlark
   who listens and rejoins,
so perhaps do mighty rivers,
   leaf buds, a boulder on its way
to smash a sunblind driver
   in a canyon, a flame
out of control, a lizard doing
   pushups on a trail near a stream
cresting. So perhaps do you
   (or I, or a bystander)
feel the urge to burst
   like milkweed, to spring
into the powder-blue dome
   of Wednesday,
in the teeth of the wind.

THE AIR IS FRESH & WILD

Throngs of greater
Sandhill cranes, dozens in a cluster,
gray-blue ghostlike bodies
stepping with tall thin legs, their ruddy
caps astonishing the dawn, some flapping,
all feeding at the verge of freezing,
on farmland curving out of town.

> *You know that slow*
> *glow-shiver*
> *inhalation of peace*
> *that comes*
> *when all the world awakes*
> *and hums? When the sky swirls blue*
> *with scrubbed white clouds*
> *and strums the distant mountains*
> *proud, with evergreens in snow?*
>
> *When flurries whirl upon the hills,*
> *and trace the petroglyphs*
> *on a sandstone face?*
> *When a solo bald eagle*
> *settles on a pole,*
> *and skews its head*
> *to gaze*
> *on you?*

Carol L. Deering

A midday fog rolls in, rain
nibbling the foothills bare, lifting a ridge,
its crest tipped in nobility, keen
as a sitting bison's back. A shaft
of light spun out of feathers
falls through the afternoon.
I take directly to the air.

SQUALL AT FISHING BRIDGE

Pelicans
        trolled the Yellowstone

wide-eyed, as rainbows
        gripped a cloud like claws.
                Bicyclists thundered on.

A hiker snapped lightning
        through a lens. And then,
                a deluge! The pelicans, stout, deliberate

white majesty on black wingtips,
        sensed the cutthroat spawn,
                plunged and skimmed the air

then sat the ripples,
        schooners in a fog. A heron
                stalked the mossy shore

contemplating frogs. Later a bear
        lumbered through our rearview mirror
                at purple nightfall. Lights

quivered and quit the cabins,
        eliciting screams. Most of the West
                stings with flame and blight

down to the struggling weeds.
        Up here, amid a drench of rain,
                all the senses ring!

                for Janet

Carol L. Deering

FREE TO ROAM

Driving south through the Rockefeller
      strip, enduring the strobe-lit

lodgepole sun,
      I thought my eyes had painted them

to ease the ache of light.
      Two black bears

jaunty and buoyant, lurched from the pines,
      sow first

bounding euphoric across the road
      a hundred yards ahead of me. Mine

      the only car around.

She was playing
      with her yearling. I slowed to nearly

nothing. The smile that sprung to my face

      shone all day.

The sheen of impenetrable beauty,
      the spunk to run and snuffle joy

across a feral home. No bluff, no grunt
      no notice of me.

I was free to roam.

MAYFLY DESTINY

Everything comes back
        to haunt or buoy us
                in the body of the night.

Choices assail us
        by the thousands
               twitching their triple tails.

In the sparkle
        of wingtips passing
                we cross the river and run

with ancient mysteries
        of rhythm and consequence,
                clambering

                        to greet the dawn.

Carol L. Deering

THE BRITTLE WORLD

Our radio rattles
incessant news, more
than flesh and blood
can bear.

We turn
onto our rut-worn road

      where a spotted fawn
month old at most

stands in the not-quite
dusk

on the brim of a quiet dirt
slope

watching our truck
draw near

      then leaps and dances
down a hidden path

to a gangly tree with family.

      This sight

inflects
the brittle world

      gives bounce
to the human race

and, for now,
the sharp-eyed
shimmery
stars

      compose themselves
in grace.

"I REST AMONG THE PEBBLE BEDS, MY HAIR IN LOOSE RACEME"

"When I am away, I anticipate my return, needing to touch stone, rock, water, the trunks of trees, the sway of grasses, the barbs of a feather, the fur left behind by a shedding bison."

Terry Tempest Williams

IN AN ABANDONED GREENHOUSE

      vines roam through my hair.
I follow cursive shadows, as lines and verses
tiger-scrawl my face. I pass impatiens
in glassed sunlight, velvet creepers
mingling begonias, sweet grapes
glistening, my shoulders spilling time. The sun

      flowers in this sprawl of fronds and climbers,
spattered, twisted, purling cabernet and green.

      Ferns in uncombed wonder
nod to nests of spider
plants, trailing fuchsia,
grasses thrumming like a harp.

      I rest among the pebble beds, my hair
in loose raceme, watching foliage and feelers
smuggle shade and shine.

      The plant above
leans into me, its leaves a flash of tongues
webbing me breathless in the scrub.

      A bearded-iris blade
scribbles a poem on my skin.

Carol L. Deering

DAYLILY PASTORALE

Plum wine, cream, twilight green,
the colors of sunrise and dew,
these blossoms ruffle, flared
and pinched, starred and ribboned,
in riotous tenderness,
ancient, yet each day new.

As one unfurls and tastes the air,
its petals cross another,
like a mare resting her head
against her foal, lingering
in a peace that ripples
straightaway to our soul.

for Roger Gose

THE BLOSSOM OF THIS AIR

Earth is a drum (all planets are).
We whirl in music as we pass.
The shush and splatter of rain,
the stones that soak up time, add melody
and fragrance to the wind. The cryptic
fire of rock responds to thunder.
Rattlesnakes snuggle in their dark.
All trees root together
to prevail. A single grain of water
speaks what the wood sparks,
what the sky provides.

Earth is a drum (circling a star).
We stomp our rhythms as we spin.
Children of the wind, stirred by eagles' wings,
see the blue sky-horse amid the clouds,
so luminous it would blind,
if it could last
for long. We stroke the convoluted
river-course of song.
        No man alone
can truly share. O why are we, then,
strangers, awkward
with the blossom of this air?

Carol L. Deering

NATURAL HISTORY

Spring surrenders to lambs and wolf pups
and every shade of green. Mountains still
in white headdresses, the clouds
roil and reel in April heartbreak,
deaf to the boisterous rush of June.

Songs of squabbling cultures rise.

Pines and willows feel a shaft of sun,
the hush of horses dreaming victory,
birds stake claim to branches, history
ready to repeat or redress.
                                        The moon
a lens on the river,
reads the weather in our eyes…

CODGE 'N SARAH'S MERCANTILE

Down a muddy roundabout highway
tucked between two stone-broke towns,
a rundown schoolhouse stirs.

Men with faces worn like wood grain
come not for peaches or tobacco
but for the companionship bartering brings.

> Kids ride the knobby horse or Sloopy
> the wall-eyed nibbling mule, or slide
> and climb on old swing frames. Parents
>
> wander the whimsical gardens
> in the spidery amethyst rain.

Codge hoists suspenders and fans harmonica
blues. Columbine lean and listen
near a willow gently swinging beads.

Carol L. Deering

Corn plants, stalks akimbo, guard
the cabbages, cut and faceted
to gems. Barrels grow lobelia, thinning like hair.

> Sarah rings a handbell. Pies rise latticed
> from a gaping oven. Everyone
> savors, then bless 'em, leaves.

> Doors shake, latch. God bless,
> Godspeed.

Codge with his bent-wood cane
tramps over scratchy hills, his beard
enflamed in the setting sun.

I'LL TAKE YOUR SILENCE

as a No. A push
aside. Busy signal. A leaf
giving up, releasing
its twig, falling away,
can't help itself

If you'll take my silence

as time, cotyledons
rising from a dead plant
in my window, as awe
doing cartwheels, spelling Yes,
spelling Wait.

Carol L. Deering

LIKE A SPIRITED SUMMER CREEK

Fifty of us troop
from the Center of Hope

>   *where tragedy blazed*
>   *a year ago*
>   *one dead, one injured, grievously*

down Main Street:
old, young, native, white,
>   one as water flows.

Near the front
in the veer and swell,
>   the light steps of a little girl

hugging a sock monkey dear.
Young boy with a hand-drawn sign:
>   "No more fighting, Stay Puft!"

Havoc & Solace

All waffed across traffic by police,
car-horn kudos from the street,
      to the band shell

cool shade of city park,
green grass, the journey
      reversing last year's course:

    park worker
    to the Center,
    feverish for gore.

      The sky
wild crayon blue, the sun
 sparking hope for conflux.
May we Stay Puft,
      and never run dry.

      for the Trosper and Goggles families,
      and for Ron Howard

Carol L. Deering

TO YOU, LAKE YELLOWSTONE

I think of you often, though we meet
but once a year. You gleam,
a countenance with a secret,
faceted ice plates framing your shore.

> You harbor countless islands, anonymous
> and named, and shudders that muse

> within the deep. You lounge in overlapping
> craters, where restless geysers snooze

and fumaroles reflect upon
their faults. Yet you rouse in beauty,
not despair, brushing the night
from your whorl of hair.

> Your tranquility calms the fire
> and wears away the ice.

Sprawling your arms throughout the park,
you can be seen from space. Like a poem,
you create the weather you want
closest to your face.

for the Thumblies

NEBRASKA DAYDREAM

Fairytale rocks grow bald in juniper.
    Cows, oil-black and limestone,
rest in tree shade, watching
    the river flex its sinews

as flowers lick the air.
    Fences wear wild grapes and roses.
Tarpaper farmhouses
    flap to the beat of a breeze.

Trees breathe softly, exhaling crows.
    On the brim of this moment,
barn-slope peace and greenful, clouds
    paddle clumsily.

The way they fracture the light,
    anything could happen … and does.

Carol L. Deering

MAGICAL RIFF

Rivers pine, no two ways
   about it. They carry luggage,
always on the run,
   spirits packed and folded,
while shadows come

               undone.

In moonlit rush
   the world's great passions
twine and spume anew,
   primal rhythms tumbling,
trembling, to overcome

               the blues.

THE FALLS

It was May and chilly, the falls

You got your first leg brace
while our son fed the geese,
trying to reach the tranquil ones,
not those who waddled up
brash and entitled
to scraps of biscuit,
but those accustomed to wait.

spewing and gathering

When he tired of that
he ran to the park
to play on an orange slide
and try all the ways to swing.

skidding down the rocks

You as a child faced
surgeries, learning to walk
three different times.
You could never run.

a long current of events

Carol L. Deering

Years ago you fell on ice.
I slipped then rose while
trying to help you stand. A man
carrying a red-haired baby
(I thought he'd ask me to hold)
scooped you upright
with his open arm,
then strolled along the road.

scurrying through the trees.

THIS DAY

Curtains parted,
            face to the glass,
I watch pale beads
            strung on a wire fence,
dark pennies dancing
            on the wet sidewalk.
Branches hold tight,
            but here and there leaves
startle and drip. Rain
            rinses the street,
weaving light and tree
            scent, calling catch me
if you can, touch me
            with your tongue. A sparkle
of songs and memories,
            a shiver of delight. This day
there is no old.

Carol L. Deering

IN A DESERT FASTNESS

where music cuts through stone,
    saguaros stretch, and teddy bear
chollas syncopate my journey
to the falls. The sun

changes seasons with its hands
    behind its back. Mallow
bobs through cow skull sockets.
    A hot breeze gestures to a hare,
shock-still, his inner ears aflame.

I stumble over rocks that thirst
    and hear their hymns of summer
frail as palo verde shade. A hawk
    stays pinned to sky-blue blaze.

Straddling boulders, I listen long:
    a wild song, water, rushing dreams
to spines and rubble, spilling
    blessings 'til the stones cry mercy.

My cup hoards the roar and shimmer.
    I slurp the zest of spring.

ON THE TRAIL

She strolls before breakfast,
beside a river of milky tea,
the morning in her pocket
like coins or fancy threadwork.

A spray of drizzle,
and sycamore branches twist
in earthy mushroom scent.
A red-breasted robin
pulls skeins of nest grasses.
Two geese overhead
go squeeze-box honking…

The river changes luster
and its mind.

A hazy ways beyond, a man
emerges from the trees,
and instantly
she becomes a woman

    alone.

Carol L. Deering

PAPER BIRCH

Its bark scrolls back,
      baring a musical staff,
hem stitching, the hush
      of paddle and canoe,
a jagged switchblade
      electrocardiogram,
the stutter of a code
      we can't quite fathom, trace
of wisdom, the paths
      we could wander
if we dared find peace.

POPO AGIE PALETTE

Hold fast to the good, the golden,
the green we carry in our heads.
Up here on dawn's horizon,
sky is whisked by falcon wings. The ledge

slopes crimson to a slender river,
sees itself through lucent eyes,
gives its every curve a shelter.
Cottonwoods shine satin. The light's awry.

Hawks float large in a twist
of wind. Go, young river, soar and stray,
recall the colors the chokecherries kissed,
the rocks and snow at the foot of your cave

the trout that, rising, sparkle at your throat.
Then let the sun down easy, amethyst to indigo ...

for Chrys,
who paints in her head

Carol L. Deering

DOWN AT TROUBLESOME CREEK

Here I stand, cow-brained in the road,
badly in need of a speck of grace,
a tug of sympathy from the cosmic
fold. Chin-whisker virgas

off towards the mesa
play at shivers of rain, sensing,
as I do, the birth of autumn
within July, a seed of pain.

A sigh of pine bough pulls me under.
I spot a private thatch of sky.
Far beyond reach in a slant of sun
spans a spider web, glistening
like a peacock feather's eye.

I see as the tree does, no need
for words. We're all related to shadows,
to the inner darkness of a bird.
Resting my palm on the old pine bark

whorls and knots shoot whispers
deep to the rivulets within,
xylem, phloem/arteries, veins,
a sprawling incandescence of kin.

Starlings like sparks
dart from a ridge quite near.
My spirit follows,
vaulting fences like a deer.

for Marilú

HELIANTHUS, HOZHO

XIT

Let's go back to that field
near Flagstaff, and watch light
push from the earth
a ray at a time, each tipped
with a flowering sun, stretching,
enriching the blue beyond.

> *That glow, rich pollen, rode with us,*
> *lightening our journey's hours.*

Once by lamplight onto leather,
you cut and beveled
a sunflower wallet, a vivid
picture of that summer, and later
of that concert, where drums, bells and strings
brightened into bloom.

The bold light of native flowers
animated yet calmed us, kept us
whole and together all these years.
When I trace the wallet with my finger
or listen to "Nihaa Shil Hozho,"
time slips back but holds us

> *in that glow, recalling "the flower*
> *that happiness grows."*

for Andy

Carol L. Deering

BLUE SKY HIGHWAY

Wind River Indian Reservation

Driving south to Ethete, you come to a long,
open curve where the land, like a jaw,
drops in awe, and even in summer
when the road is dry,
but chiefly in winter
with packed snow and ice,
causes you brief disquiet

as you tap the brake. You feel lifted
straight to the sky, towards
the snow-swirled mountains,
luring and lofting you
across the abyss, through the whispers
of blood and fire. You could fly,
look down, and drop. But

you tighten your grip,
trace the wild curve, then
roll down the road, stunned
and humbled,
gratefully whole.

for Scott Momaday

REMINISCENCE

This jacquard-patterned river,
pulling up
its socks, tripping, scampering, leaping
shadows,
plays with threads of light,
running
tiptoe, allegretto con moto,
jaunty
with all its might.

The snow on the bank
glows blue
and ponderous,
all the full moon

long.

Carol L. Deering

STORIES ON THE WIND

Bear Lodge (Devils Tower)

Some say the tower was born of fire
(as poems are, deep in the throat
before words), longing to burst
and spend its glory, to forfeit all
to performance and ash. No one knows
what choked that flourish, locking
a heart in consummate stone.

Some say raindrops and the river,
freezing and thawing, wore down
the fragile rock and soil,
exposing the tower flame-naked to dawn.
Without the restless swirl
of the river, the rain so patient but
eager to cleanse, no one could ever
foresee a tower
hidden fast within that land.

Havoc & Solace

Some say the rock rose up for children
as a massive bear clawed out in vain.
A Great Spirit gathered
the terror-stricken sisters,
clustering them far-flung in space.
Some invoke this spirit
with charms on branches wound
in feather bundles,
essence of prayer on the wind.

I say, from all my wanderings,
talk to the ponderosa. Their roots
scrape the soil and boulders,
their branches taste the wind and sway
to prehistoric fire, water,
poetry and prayer. They trumpet their stories
from the planet's molten core
to a bright bouquet of stars
beyond the grasp of bears.

Carol L. Deering

MIDNIGHT, MARCH

Lady with a margarita,
   legs crossed,
dressed in flowers
   waits in vain.

Her hair cascades
   from a slim barrette,
her smoke dancing
   to the ache of a minor key.

Another freight train
   thunders past, another
glass, a cigarette
   twisting in its tray.

She's fashioned herself
   a tree from splinters,
a twig where tenor sax
   takes flight. Lady

with a margarita,
   vitality and pain,
inflorescence on the night,
   fabricating spring.

"DIRT, OUR COMMON SKIN, OUR RICH IDENTITY IN SPACE"

"It is a lucky part of the world;
to grow old without buildings
and roadways,
to dissolve quietly
without feeling stunned."

Naomi Shihab Nye

WE NAMED OUR PLANET

for its dirt. Earth, we said,
come let us toil and rest.

Down to earth, we say,
when someone's grounded,
solid citizen, digging up the soil.

Loam falls through our fingers,
    till
       plant
    till.

Bowls of dust visit us,
    day
       after
    day.

Gold dust, boom or bust,
dirt, our common skin,
our rich identity in space.

Stars are born
from gas and dust, comets
from dirt and ice.

Here we sit, dazzled by dirt,
little moons
reflecting in our eyes.

NEVADA SANDS

froth and break
like sea spray
crashing,
like a heart
with nothing

left to lose.

Carol L. Deering

LIGHT PHYSICS

The quarter moon
proclaims her silver sprawl
a dancefloor,
a meeting place for pronghorn,
rabbits, an occasional
skim of birds, anyone
drawn to sand and tension,
soft vibration,
out of the cougar wind,
night
sensing that light
is music, and music
humming its shadows dense,
whispered cadence
embraced
by light.

NAVAJO MOON

The moon
an evening primrose,
watchful and profound,
unfurls. The desert, a pink-to-azure
splash, warms itself in campfire spurs
to the chilly edge.

We clasp
a mano, stone memory of corn
and metate, chanced upon a rock shelf,
worn and smoothed through centuries
of rhythmic grinding
under spirited skies.
We weigh the past

and present,
talk of coal-fired towers stalking
this powerful land, how people
grind on one another. Hush
of twilight's indigo thirst. Hills
draw close on their knees.
A breeze tassels out as we replace

the stone.
Night, a panoramic pictograph,
records the old and new: golden dazzle
firelight, ritual prayers for crops
and rain, moonlit towers
chanting, corn pollen scattering.
Cedar starburst.

This sacred plain.

Carol L. Deering

THE AUGUST WEST

Sun comes out, all wrists
and elbows above its head,
hung over and closing its eyes
in pain, its solo muffled
behind a scarf of smoke. It's
that time of year; all the suns
are wearing one, and forests
dress in skins of flame.

WE WERE THE PURPLE DISTANCE

Yellowstone, 1988

i.
Lightning chose a single tree
in the driest summer of a century,
then kept on striking, a rattlesnake
disturbed, a many-headed monster
with a bold blue heart. Pines
jumped crimson
out of feathered greenery,
sighed and mingled, kindling delirium.
Smoke plumes gulped down air. Wind
skimmed shriveled grasses, as branches
burned and flew apart, like birds.

No loon, no maniacal laughter
over water.

Night and day, week after week,
insatiable storms whirled
rocks and brush around,
breathed in, breathed out
as tempers flared. Helicopters
poured the river onto the forest. Elk
nibbled bark, and bison licked the ash.
Ghostly embers coasted in the breeze.

How odd that fire sounds like rain.
What smells they each rip open.

Carol L. Deering

ii.
We were the purple distance,
tousled on a fringe of storm. No
bright, no shade, all muslin sky
sheathing a bold red globe. Passive
smokers with painful eyes. A spark
and a child was born,
breathed in, breathed out
night and day, week after week,
toddler to teen, as joy
and tempers flared.

No crane dancing, legs
acute and jumping, to distract us.

*Fire and water in our hearts.
Wild storms dwindle and whirl.*

Havoc & Solace

iii.
Logs are alligator-charred these days.
Sagebrush sputters
black within fresh grasses,
fireweed, and fire-sown pines. Aspen
breed in crooked pathways.

Clark's nutcrackers
stash the seeds from fallen cones.
Whole stands of unscathed lodgepole
listen, as rivers recite their tales
of flying and falling from great height,
the courage it took
to embrace the inescapable heat.

Geyser steam distorts yet clarifies.
  Sunlit leaves rejoice.

> *in memory of Riley Mitchell,*
> *former Chief of Interpretation*
> *at Devils Tower National Monument*
> *and Capitol Reef National Park*

Carol L. Deering

INDIAN RICEGRASS

Light skitters across the white, white
misty-looking grass
in our neighbors' pasture. It's not
swaying this May morning –

    Nothing is…

but you know it's the softest,
driest, angel-wing grass
left
on earth.

    A spark could shout this land aflame.

The field may get mowed
this summer, since they no longer
keep horses. Wind and rain
will tap and sweep
or flirt.

    Nothing you can do…

Its wispy, whispery beauty
in this delicate, eerie light
warms and cuts
straight through your heart.

MUD BUBBLES & BREATHES

<u>THEN</u>: *Molten rocks*
          slithered like lizards
          beneath the tumult,
          rain and snowmelt.

<u>NOW</u>: *Fountain Paint Pot*
          hot mud alive,
          bulbous faces breed then dive,
          bullfrog bubbles plop! squish! suck!
          open big mouths, then swallow up.

Superheated water
          plum mocha, cocoa-gray,
          viscous gases gurgle, falter,
          lobbing mud in hoodoo play.

Spurt of ripples and rings,
          abstract artists daub and slop,
          turntable music, clay soup oozing,
          whirlpools struggle, slap, and sing.

Carol L. Deering

<u>SOON</u>: *Supervolcano*
         magma cache,
         walls of lava fill the caldera,
         blowing all to giddy ash.
         Groundless rumors frown,
         open big mouths, then swallow down.

<u>STILL</u>: *Something wriggles*
         in this water, fated
         to roil and mourn,
         toiling in this fetid
         slime, waiting to be born…

                        for Suki

IN THE BALANCE

We were late to begin with.
A man named Wisdom
brimmed with invitation
to a Hopi butterfly dance,
a sacred ceremony
on a sandy byway down the road.
Every pueblo around the plaza
would feed us. We were honored
and yearned to go.

> We pondered this golden chance,
> glowing with hope, shoving our clothes
> into bags zipped and stacked
> against the plaid ambivalence
> of the room. It would be beautiful,
> slow reverence unspooling, time
> forever calm.

We had to be long gone by noon.

> Our van was low to the ground,
> we knew, and a truck or a bus
> could park in the space
> for the ramp. Your chair
> would balk in the sand. By sad
> default we chose the canyon rim,
> the frenzied thoroughfare.

Carol L. Deering

You settled into the van's
front seat. I sat on the curb,
feet in the dirt, blue shadow
basking in Moenkopi warmth,
Wisdom's appeal.
Blessing enough, for now.

DAWN TO DUSK, A LIFESPAN

Sky-blue pink, the sun
      bold behind a golden-green
      lace of cottonwood,
stretches this October day.

Smoke-lined clouds
      yawn across the scene. Horses
      never turn from their buckets
but register a chill.

I stroll down the road, the breath
      of a tree on my neck, the spangles
      and all their yearnings
a chorus in my blood.

      My phone blasts: a shooting
            at my former college. Police
            have the gunman in custody,
      no details
                 so far.

Our pitiless time
      on this skin of earth
      grows cold, a rock, dried stalks
waving for their lives.

Carol L. Deering

BROKEN WEAVE

Wrapped in wings of a floured apron
a woman settles into time-frayed comfort,
her hands a nest for steaming chocolate,
lavender brown in an old ceramic mug.

Beyond the dusty bedsheet curtains,
dry leaves, like penny-colored horses,
ride the shaggy wind,
join the tumbleweed migration
across the rugged land. Her brow
regards the land she's knit,
the land she's struggled kneading –
land that holds its people, for awhile.

The tapestry of the moment
as the screens go violet
admits no poverty of feeling.
Inside this house she's fashioned,
plaster strengthened with her hair,
the woman sips the bittersweet
and cups despair.

HARVEST WHIMSY

Birds, berserk, thrash into windows.

    Branches carve the house.

Thoughts sprawl, misshapen

    pumpkins in a field. All this raking,

canning, gleaning, wild

    shivering as autumn trundles in,

yields to whimsy and pretend.

    Trees sigh free of fresher leaves,

fiery topaz sacrifices

    twining the purple-black

sickle throat of Wind.

Carol L. Deering

SOMEWHERE WEST OF LARAMIE

Sun blinds the fractured
windshield. Cloistered within,
all music clasps its praise.
The steering wheel poses
at awkward angles,
a medal for bravery, unwavering
against the trauma behind.

> *That night we spun 180,*
> *black ice, and then black eye.*
> *Time split and looked down crooked.*
> *We wriggled from windows*
> *and watched a wheel set course*
> *for a canyon filled with stars.*

Wanton grasses rustle
from the hollows of old tires.
This parched warrior, now wracked
with silent battle cries, rocked
and rolled to landscape rubble,
where snakes and packrats worship
and men with wrenches prey.

ANGLE OF INCIDENCE

Something's off-balance
in the air, throbbing me
unclear.

> *I spoke softly,*
> *plain as day, yet we parted*
> *lonesome as dusk.*
>
> *Silence occupied your ears.*
>
> *Other eyes slid past me,*
> *spent no notice,*
> *or held so slow*
>
> *I longed to disappear.*

Little birds on roadside stalks
rise and shiver to a mist,
shying me to tears.

Carol L. Deering

PASSAGE

A curbstone is a wall,
  as are thresholds, steps,
    a space too tiny to wheel
      around in, a gate too tall

        to reach across, a mass of
          fallen snow. But riding frost
            on a ramp freshly shoveled
              pops and crackles like applause.

THE SAME WIND, LIGHT & RESTLESS RAIN

Thick mist rides
this sluggish river, suspending Rez
and white. We people
face each other, shoot
straight up like rabbits
and run. Our minds
ruffle and burn,
stop reasoning,
contending for the sun.

> *We live on land*
> *long loved*
> *and tended.*
> > *The wind*
> > *still fans historic fire.*

We crave the light, blue sky,
the clouds and shadow edges
we share, to see how cultures fit
together, define respect
and treat despair. To halt
the raging somersault
of violence and pain.

> *The same wind, light,*
> *and restless rain*
> *sustain us.*
> > *Show me*
> > *the rain in your eyes.*

Carol L. Deering

The twisted language,
treaty lies, a froth
of winter, bitter
on all sides.
Our hearts ache and wear,
our homes filled with fear,
yesterday
a vulture at our bones.

> *We need to talk,*
> *face forward, listen*
> *to the tone.*
> *   And breathe*
> *each other's air.*

THE MILE-HIGH WEST

Today
the sky's blue purpose
is to tantalize, to write back
into our hearts what we've lost
in winter, before new spring
can color its birds. The bare trees
lean at full attention. Parched shrubs
and grasses ripple in a gust
all their own. The only bird,
dark against a slender cloud.

Carol L. Deering

WIND'S APOLOGY

Last night, and before, the wind
wrapped a ribbon around and
around our house, a noisy
process, rapping and wrapping.
Tonight it's silent, and sleeping

is truly a gift. But, look!
The sky is polished
obsidian. If you could run
your finger around the horizon,
it would sing like a bowl.

ACKNOWLEDGEMENTS

My sincere thanks to the editors of the following journals and anthologies for taking a chance on these poems (or their earlier configurations):

JOURNALS:
Algebra of Owls: "Angle of Incidence."
All Arts Newsletter [Wyoming Arts Council]: "Broken Weave."
Bindweed Magazine: "Reminiscence."
Cholla Needles Magazine: "Harvest Whimsy," "Phrynosoma Douglassii," "Quill Shine," "To You, Lake Yellowstone."
Colorado North Review: "In an Abandoned Greenhouse."
The Crow Literary Journal: "The Brittle World" (as "Gambol & Glow"), "Codge 'n Sarah's Mercantile."
EarthSpeak Magazine: "Mayfly Destiny."
Gyroscope Review: "We Named Our Planet."
The High Plains Register: "Call & Response," "Helianthus, Hozho," "Nevada Sands."
I-70 Review: "Squall at Fishing Bridge."
The Kerf: "Interchange, Wyoming" (as "Interchange"), "Natural History," "Paper Birch."
Kingdoms in the Wild: "The Same Wind, Light & Restless Rain."
The Long Island Literary Journal: "The Falls."
Matter: "Somewhere West of Laramie."
NatureWriting: "Stopping at Louis Lake."
New Limestone Review: "Free To Roam."
Oakwood Literary Magazine: "Light Physics."
Open Window Review: "Whenever I Brake for Deer" (as "I Brake for Deer"), "Let It Be."
The Paddock Review: "A Flurry of Horses."
Pentimento Magazine: "Passage" (as "Passageway").
Prairie Wolf Press Review: "A Few Seconds Eye-to-Eye."
RavensPerch Literary Magazine: "Dawn to Dusk, a Lifespan," "Midnight, March."
Rio Grande Review: "The Blossom of This Air" (as "To Taste the Wind"), "In a Desert Fastness."
Riversongs: "Wind's Apology."

Sin Fronteras Journal/Writers without Borders: "I'll Take Your Silence."
Sky Island Journal: "Blue Sky Highway."
Soundings Review: "The August West."
Sow's Ear Poetry Review: "On the Trail."
Spiral Notebook Musings: "Nebraska Daydreams" (as "Nebraska Pastorale").
Star 82: "In the Balance."
Sugar Mule 44: Women Writing Nature: "Daylily Pastorale," "Down at Troublesome Creek," "Magical Riff."
Third Wednesday: "This Day."
The Weekly Avocet: "The Air Is Fresh & Wild."
Westering: "Twilight, Angus."
WyoPoets newsletter: "The Air Is Fresh & Wild," "Broken Weave," "Daybreak, Jackson Lake," "Popo Agie Palette."
Zoomorphic: "Alchemy."

ANTHOLOGIES:
Blood, Water, Wind, & Stone: An Anthology of Wyoming Writers. Lori Howe, Ed. (Sastrugi Press, 2016): "Natural History."
Flint-Edged Refrains. Lee Ann Siebken, Ed. (WyoPoets, 2000): "Stories on the Wind."
Howl of the Wild. John Dixon, Ed. (Winterwolf Press, 2017): "Squall at Fishing Bridge."
Ring of Fire: Writers of the Yellowstone Region. Bill Hoagland, Ed. (Rocky Mountain Press, 2000): "Homespun," "Twilight, Angus."
Small Town Poetry Anthology. Tom Montag & David Graham, Eds. (MWPH Books [Midwestern Writers Publishing House], 2018): "Like a Spirited Summer Creek."
Weather Watch: Poems from Wyoming. Barbara M. Smith, Ed. (WyoPoets, 2014): "A Flurry of Horses."
Wyoming: Prairies, Peaks and Skies. Lou Layman, Ed. (WyoPoets, 1998): "Leupp Road Crossing" (as "Cycle Vision").
Wyoming Promises. Nancy Curtis, Ed. (High Plains Press, 1984): "Homespun."
Wyoming Writing: An Anthology of Winning Entries in Wyoming Writers' Contests. (Wyoming Writers, 1984, 1994): "Broken Weave," "Navajo Moon" (as "Navajo Twilight").

NOTES

Page 12: **"Phrynosoma Douglassii"**: In Sunset Crater Volcanic National Monument, near Flagstaff, this short-horned lizard (or horned toad) has adapted its coloration over the years to blend with its surroundings.

Page 24: **"Free To Roam"**: The John D. Rockefeller Jr. Memorial Parkway connects Grand Teton and Yellowstone National Parks. Wildlife and traffic roam between.

Page 39: **"Nebraska Daydream"**: North of Chimney Rock National Historic Site.

Page 41: **"The Falls"**: Idaho Falls, mid-1990s.

Page 44: **"In a Desert Fastness"**: White Tank Mountain Regional Park, west of Phoenix.

Page 47: **"Popo Agie Palette"**: Sinks Canyon State Park, Wyoming. "Popo Agie" [*pron. puh-pó-shuh*], a Crow word that many believe means "gurgling water," is the name of a river which sinks underground through a cave, then rises down the road.

Page 50: **"Blue Sky Highway"** passes through Ethete, on the Wind River Indian Reservation. Kiowa writer N. Scott Momaday, the first Native American to win the Pulitzer Prize (for his novel *House Made of Dawn*, 1969), visited Fremont County with his daughter Jill in 2009. He spoke and read at Central Wyoming College and at several Reservation schools. I was honored to be his driver.

Page 52: **"Stories on the Wind"**: This poem began at Devils Tower National Monument (Bear Lodge) where I was awarded a writer's residency, a joint venture of the National Park Service and the Bear Lodge Writers, of Sundance.

Page 59: **"Navajo Moon"**: The desert around Page, Arizona, many years ago.

Page 72: **"Somewhere West of Laramie"**: Title of an old Jordan motor car ad which ends: "Then start for the land of real living … into the red horizon of a Wyoming twilight."

Page 75: **"The Same Wind, Light & Restless Rain"**: The Wind River Indian Reservation (Arapaho and Shoshone) and the City of Riverton ~ an ongoing border dispute…

THANKS

This book has taken years to coalesce. There were days I could have given up, but confidence arrives on tiny footsteps. Thanks to the West Thumb Poets (Betsy Bernfeld, Lynne Bama, Jazmyn McDonald, Mary Robinson, and, for a long time, Janet S. Meury), Tom Spence, James McKean, Kathleen Condon, Dell Harney, Echo Klaproth & the Westword Writers, the Work Group years ago, and Marilú Duncan. To WyoPoets and Wyoming Writers, each of which offers exceptional programs and camaraderie. To Barbara Gose for her confidence, encouragement, and friendship.

And to my husband, Andy, for his capacity for wonder, his deep interest in nature, and for all his patience and love.

Winning the 2016 Wyoming Arts Council Poetry Fellowship gave me the final push I needed to labor and fuss over this collection. Most of the poems submitted for the fellowship are included in this book. And I'm deeply indebted to Rebecca Foust, the judge, for encouraging me to finish it!

Last but not least, I want to thank Lori Howe, my editor, for her insight and thoughtfulness. It was a pleasure to work with her.

ABOUT THE AUTHOR

Carol L. Deering was born and grew up in New England but has lived well over half her life in the inland West, specifically western Wyoming, northern and southern Arizona, and east-of-the-Cascades Washington. The poems in this book are inspired by these wild and rural lands, and her travels around, through, and between. They are, above all, poems of connection: animal, plant, rivers, people, rock, snow ~ nature and culture in many incarnations.

Carol holds a BA in English from Springfield College, and an MA in Librarianship & Information Management from the University of Denver. After a lifetime of library work she has settled into full-time writing. She has twice received the Wyoming Arts Council Poetry Fellowship (2016, judge Rebecca Foust; 1999, judge Agha Shahid Ali).

Her poetry appears in online and traditional journals, such as *The High Plains Register, Pinyon, Rio Grande Review, Prairie Wolf Press Review,* and *Owen Wister Review,* and in the anthologies *Ring of Fire: Writers of the Yellowstone Region* (Rocky Mountain Press) and the recent *Blood, Water, Wind & Stone: An Anthology of Wyoming Writers* (Sastrugi Press).

She and her husband live in Wyoming. This is her first book.

www.caroldeering.com

"No man alone
can truly share. O why are we, then,
strangers, awkward
with the blossom of this air?"

Other Books by Sastrugi Press

2024 Total Eclipse State Series by Aaron Linsdau
Sastrugi Press has published state-specific guides for the 2024 total eclipse crossing over the United States. Check the Sastrugi Press website for the available state eclipse books:
www.sastrugipress.com/eclipse

50 Wildlife Hotspots by Moose Henderson
Find out where to find animals and photograph them in Grand Teton National Park from a professional wildlife photographer. This unique guide shares the secret locations with the best chance at spotting wildlife.

A Small Pile of Feathers by Gerry Spence
Gerry Spence reveals his spiritual, loving, and sometimes humorous sides, depicted in his devotion to family and preserving the wild places he writes of as though they were inscribed on his own bones and in his own blood.

Along the Sylvan Trail by Julianne Couch
Along the Sylvan Trail dips into the lives of linked characters as they confront futures that aren't clearly dictated by conventional planning. The conflicts of the small town change and pressure residents of Sylvan Grove to look beyond their world to the outside.

Antarctic Tears by Aaron Linsdau
What would make someone give up a high-paying career to ski alone across Antarctica to the South Pole? This inspirational true story will make readers both cheer and cry. Fighting skin-freezing temperatures, infections, and emotional breakdown, Aaron Linsdau exposes the harsh realities of being on an expedition.

Cache Creek by Susan Marsh
Five minutes from the hubbub of Jackson's town square, Cache Creek offers the chance for hikers to immerse themselves in wild nature. It is a popular hiking, biking, and cross-country ski area on the outskirts of Jackson, Wyoming.

Cloudshade by Lori Howe, Ph.D.
The poems of *Cloudshade* breathe with the vivid, fragrant essence of life in every season on America's high plains. Extraordinarily relatable, the poems of *Cloudshade* swing wide a door to life in the West, both for lovers of poetry and for those who don't normally read poems.

Diary of a Dude Wrangler by Struthers Burt
The dude ranch world of Struthers Burt was a romantic destination in the early twentieth century. They transported people back to the Wild West. These ranches were and still are popular destinations. Experience the old west through this dude rancher's writing.

Is It True? by Eugene Gagliano
This delightful collection of children's humorous poetry encourages parents to interact in an enjoyable way with their children, to help them understand the many misunderstandings of common expressions used in our daily language.

Journeys to the Edge by Randall Peeters, Ph.D.
What is it like to climb Mount Everest? It requires dreaming big and creating a personal vision to climb the mountains in your life. Randall Peeters shares his successes and failures and gives you some directly applicable guidelines on how to create a life vision.

Lost at Windy Corner by Aaron Linsdau
Windy Corner on Denali has claimed lives, fingers, and toes. What would make someone brave lethal weather, crevasses, and slick ice to attempt to summit North America's highest mountain? The author shares the lessons Denali teaches on managing goals and risks. Apply the message, build resilience, and overcome adversities in your life.

Prevailing Westerlies by Ed Lavino
With clarity and intensity, Ed Lavino's photographs express a longing for the natural world and hope for its future through his black and white photography.

Roaming the Wild by Grover Ratliff
Experience the landscape and wildlife photography of Grover Ratliff in this unique volume. Jackson Hole is home to some of the most iconic landscapes in North America. In this land of harsh winters and short summers, wildlife survives and thrives.

Sleeping Dogs Don't Lie by Michael McCoy
A young Native American boy is taken from his home after tragedy strikes, grows up in middle America, and through his first real adult summer searches for Wyoming artifacts, falls in with the subversive Dog Soldiers Resurrected, and attempts single-handedly to solve the murder of his treasured coworker.

So I Said by Gerry Spence
The collected sayings of Gerry Spence provokes readers into thinking about their own vision of the world. As a lawyer with decades of experience in defending the defenseless, he's fought against giants. His insights provide a grander vision of how the nearly invisible world of the justice system in *So I Said*.

Voices at Twilight by Lori Howe, Ph.D.
Voices at Twilight is a guide takes readers on a visual tour of twelve past and present Wyoming ghost towns. Contained within are travel directions, GPS coordinates, and tips for intrepid readers.

Visit Sastrugi Press on the web at www.sastrugipress.com to purchase the above titles in bulk. They are available from your local bookstore or online retailers in print, e-book, or audiobook form.

Thank you for choosing Sastrugi Press.
www.sastrugipress.com
"Turn the Page Loose"

www.ingramcontent.com/pod-product-compliance
Lightning Source LLC
Chambersburg PA
CBHW031943070426
42450CB00006BA/801